# Rain, Sky, Wind, Port

# Rain, Sky, Wind, Port

Poems

Kim Nam-Jo

*Translations by*
*Hillel Schwartz & Sunny Jung*

A Forsythia Book

Codhill Press
New Paltz, New York

THIS IS A CODHILL BOOK

Codhill books are published by David Appelbaum for Codhill Press



ISBN 1-930337-76-0
First Edition

This publication was made possible in part by the generous support
of the Literature Translation Institute of Korea (LTI Korea).

Book Design by Alicia Fox
Cover art © Alicia Fox
www.aliciafoxdesign.com

Library of Congress Cataloging-in-Publication Data

Kim, Nam-jo, 1927–
[Poems. Selections English]
Rain, sky, wind, port : poems / Kim Nam-Jo ;
Translations by Hillel Schwartz & Sunny Jung. — First Edition.
p. cm
Translated Korean poems into English.
Includes bibliographical references and index.
ISBN 1-930337-76-0 (alk. paper)
I. Schwartz, Hillel, 1948– translator. II. Jung, Sunny, translator. III. Title.

PL992.415.N3A6 2014
895.714—dc23

2014012749

## Table of Contents

## 1. Scribble

"No regrets, I'm getting old."
        (What else is new?)
First line.

"I was granted the glory of a soul."
        (But can there be a soul that does no justice to that glory?)
Second line.

How presumptuous of me!
Born without tariff,
every day in this world undeserved,
yet I dare to covet
the best of what is humanly possible,
crying for the moon.

## 2. Companion

Under the dim light in the night train
I'm sure that you and I have been together.
Front seat or back or next seat over,
you must always have been there.
When I rested my tired body on its far travels
or was elbowing my way through a crowd
in the strange haste of loneliness,
there too I'm sure I had a glimpse of you.

When I've hesitated
along the ordinary course of my life
or fumbled toward the core of things,
I'm sure that someone always helped me.
Someone always brushed across
the solitary path of my heart.
I'm sure it was you.
Thus I became a sensitive instrument
that could be played by the hint of a breeze.

So now
I dedicate to you this table entire,
its food and perfect setting,
with the whole weight of my life behind it.
O my dear, you who have been my love for so long!
Today, in the full light of a white sun, I welcome you
as we bow together, bride and groom.

## 3. To My Poem 4

"I am no poet.
I am someone begging for poems."
This used to be my true confession.

More than once,
holding up a white flag,
I have given in, saying
"I surrender. I surrender."

While you took your pleasure to the fullest,
roaming the mountains and rivers,
I was the one on the lam,
vagabonding through foreign lands,
a habitual and total loser.
For this I apologize,
and repent.

Finally
an expert at unrequited love
and well-versed in your long absences,
now,

O Poem!
as you reveal yourself to me ever so faintly,
my heart begins to pound and once again
I reach out my arms toward you,
enraptured.

## 4. Winter Flowers

1
Hugged to a breast and carried along a snowy road,
a bunch of flowers.
Snow brushed off, you are stretched out to me.
Half ice,
and hot! burning with life,
fire-seeds hidden
within each frozen layer of skin,
aching, throbbing with cold...
the flower-light dazzles me.

2
At last I am relieved.
Crying in front of you,
I become human again.

Before you,
winter flowers,
beaming even with your stalks cut
and frosted leaves crunching,
my tears, so long dry, now well up
and I become human again.

## 5. Trees 5

O Trees!
Enduring such burdens,
unfolding fruit like birds' nests
and watching over them, watching tenderly over them,
unsleeping even at night.

Swaying and sagging with fruit
grown large and provident,
lift up those branches!
Lift them up!
Massive sun in mid-sky:
your flesh.

Your joy is most exactly that burden,
O Trees!
Blood and flesh swelling,
the more swollen the fruit the greater your resilience
and more splendid your power.

Today,
fruit harvested,
you let fall your leaves.

## 6. Trees 7

From the start, trees study how to stand,
how to look off in the distance as they grow,
how to accommodate any weather.
And when trees learn they cannot cuddle with one another,
they study how to wave to each neighbor in blue and green.

Trees live to study:
how to pump water through their roots,
how to greet all things one by one—
the farthest sky, clouds,
wildflowers, insects among the grasses,
and their most delicate brothers.
Their shadows too, they study their shadows,
and how to offer shelter to wanderers,
how to use their canopies to screen the sun.

Even at night, trees study:
as the sun sets and night deepens,
then too they uncover the beauty of the world
and the fact that on any given day
or through any night, no one is alone,
or far from any other.

## 7. Winter Laundry

Across the chill of a drift
the ardent morning sun, still unfolding,
throws itself down on its knees
as if to pray.
All night long
snow had washed the world as white
as the fresh laundry that lit the darkness.

Uncanny,
how even the shadows of garments
hanging from washlines over the snow—
purest white on purest white, overlapping ever so lightly—
seem to me alive and responsive,
how everywhere
a cool freshness and brightness
unkinks the knots within this world
and combs them out.
All that is left has a certain softness.

Among the humdrum of daily life
beauties
rapturous, overwhelming,
move a person to applaud
the spirits of the place.
Snow and sun are pleased with themselves
in what seems to be heaven's country
and the least I can do is stand aside,
make no shadow.

## 8. Tear

When I want to see a tear
I sit in front of the t.v.
and watch a children's show.
In moving images of classic children's stories,
there is extraordinary beauty
when a good child grows sad.
A translucent blue-glass tear
takes shape
and a strange glass thread
slips down across the cheek.

Shaken by wind,
the dew inside a flower
reflects God's country.
I can understand this, and I know
my heart once again
has been clarified.
And I think, this world is a good place,
a really good place.

## 9. Famine, That Story

Once, in a poor monastery,
a man ate four times more than the others,
who had so little they came close to starving.
Later, to their surprise,
all met again in heaven,
the glutton among them.

Said God:
"Because he ate only a quarter of the food
to which his great hunger entitled him
and left the rest to others,
my compassion has been aroused
and I have summoned him here to praise him."

This drew belly laughs
from the celestial audience
but all soon fell quiet.

Here below the situation is desperate.
See: the piercing hunger
each has for someone else
and our insatiable appetite for something more.

## 10. Combing My Hair

I am combing my hair.
Combing tonight with a passion
as if combing out uncountable threads
of darkness.

Does a sleek jet-black light glisten
through each rich strand of hair
because human thoughts are so dark?

I pour more oil in the stove.
The pure flame, burning, calls out,
as in a scene where two spirits meet,
        each knowing full well
        what it is to be faithful,
and embrace for eternity.

Mankind has a history of ideas
that shone with possibility like the leftover light of dawn
then guttered out in firepits,
and no one can say the time was too short
to learn exactly what it means to be faithful.

Tonight
I am combing my long hair
as if softly combing out the fin of a fish of the abysses
under immense pressure.
I am cold like a woman sent packing.

## 11. After That

After that,
tell me,
what happened to you?

If you spurn words,
show me in my dreams in deepest night
with picture books
whose leaves I may turn page by page.
Ring me up, my ear a phone,
and let me hear the sound
of clothes rustling,
doors opening and closing.

I want blinding clarity,
all the usual senses keenly alert,
and all of my other senses, too.
Like Andersen's match girl.
lighting each and every match for tinder,
I would be awake
a thousand nights.

Please, let me know:
After that,
what happened to you?
In that world
is there any breast on which at last,
cold and desolate,
you can take comfort?
Are you finally in peace?

Send at least your regards. Please.

Can you fathom
how my longing and regret
keep growing like new crops filling a great field?

Please let me know
by wireless or even by satellite.
Please, let me know.

## 12. Last Letter

Sealed my last letter
but couldn't send it.
Though the four seasons have danced through several circles
and shaken dew from their bare feet,
it's not yet time to scrape off
ink-black tattoos from white skin,
not yet time to shed my clothes.

Like streams that pass through sloughs
and change their mud-red clothes over and over
to become rivers clear as crystal,
wind and sun and the hearts of men and women
spin out long skeins of yarn,
paying the debt on a million troubles,
until all that remains is love.

Even though this letter
contains one such love story,
it's not yet time to send it.
The letter lies intact
and neatly tucked within its seal of wax.
Ah! My so old but forever young
last letter.

## 13. Door

Their long journey continues.

'Til now, they have gone through the fortunes
of many days across a multitude of mountains and rivers.
The skein of silk has been all spun out, the silkworm exhausted.
Sand has flown through an hourglass, *baseuk-baseuk*
a trillion grains of sand, run out.

'Til now they have passed exit doors large and small;
passed the last exit too.
I assure you:
they have already passed the last exit.

Their long journey continues.
Some day, no doubt,
they will come to a place
with yet another door
opening onto the next world.

## 14. Trees and Shadows

Trees and shadows.
Trees look down upon shadows.
Shadows look up toward trees.
Even as night settles,
even as rain descends
shadows are there.
Trees know it.

## 15. To the Wind

Wind,
now that you have made it here,
don't you want a sabbatical?

Wind!
All you ever did was run
and make farewells.
No one on her own
could have done what you did,
globetrotting and learning the world,
bruised and sick with vertigo.
Now you have come to a standstill,
frozen after brushing your lips
over hills of frost, ice-flower trees,
and facets of cold crystal.

Sky
a cotton cloth,
washed and laundered.
Weather,
snow falling like finely-ground salt.
Wind, stuck here with me,
can you not, as never before,
lie down and stretch out?

Wind,
wind
wearing a glass dress.
O wind!

## 16. Days of Wounded Soldiers

During my days as a wounded soldier
another wounded soldier
lay in the next bed over,
so I was grateful.

When yet another soldier
was brought in, wounded
for a second time,
I was also grateful.

As time passed
and the wounded grew thick around me—
the next bed over always occupied—
I was always grateful.

I grew accustomed to the wounded
whoever and however they were
as days of pain offset by days of ease
evened out toward calmer weather,
for which I was most thankful.

In other words,
when you were wounded
I was there with you,
my friend.

## 17. Peace

If anyone wants to call him,
whispering is not enough.
Nor is singing as in a lullaby.
Instead, roar like a lion: O Peace!
No, louder. *O Peace!*
You must call out, shaking like thunder.

With noble carriage, great dignity,
and surpassing beauty,
he is everyone's lover,
the finest human on both sides of the millennium.
*O Peace, O Peace, please come!*
Risking blood-bruises,
with all of your strength
you must call his name.

But merely calling his name
he might not come.
Taking up the spoons and chopsticks left behind
by brothers who died in a world never peaceful enough,
and sharing their unfinished bread and hope,
and eating our own bread and hope too,
when in the name of humankind
we confess a love more than love,
*—O Peace! O Holy Heart!—*
inevitably he will come.

## 18. Even in the Acid Rain

[Acid snow is falling.
I almost said, "How beautiful. . . ."]

O the despair of a poet!
In my heart, too, all winter long
the acid snow fell.

This spring season
acid rain has fallen several times,
its acidity so intense
it eats through metal.
The newspapers say it has fallen
in Yongsan, Sangmoondong, Myunmokdong.

What can I do about this acid rain?
What can I do indeed
for rows of young plants
with bare heads and bare feet,
for the first light green shoots of spring,
clear as tears,
budding and sprouting,
and for our children
under the rain?

Oh, bright April!
Such an abundance of blossoms . . .
ah, ah, wash your eyes, splash your face with acid rain
and after that acid bath—
like that blind man in the Bible
who was told by Jesus
to wash his eyes with mud
and once he did he saw—
praise God.

What can I do
with feelings so profoundly at odds?

## 19. Mirror Inside the Mirror

For the first time, from early light,
in the company of an old friend, Sorrow,
and strains of familiar music—
*Mirror Inside the Mirror—*
I study the falling rain.

No:
rather, I am drawn endlessly,
hour upon hour, to watch the rain as it falls,
listening still to a melody programmed to repeat,
a melody that seems the very soul of music.

And the way I live now
feels like some counterpart life,
a life in parallel.

The rain falls straight.
It splits the pleated surfaces of shallow pools,
small wet obelisks dissolving
the moment they take shape.

The rain slips down across my window
in slanting rivulets
long, thin, and fine as threads of white gold.

Never have I seen so many tears,
tears that flow naturally after a rain.
Correction: these are more dramatic tears,
tears of relief and release, tears of the lonely,
like a chorus weeping in unison.

It's gotten dark,
and every oil lamp in the world
is being filled once more with sacred paraffin.

## 20. To the Mountains and the Trees

The mountains couldn't come to me
so I went to the mountains.
The trees couldn't come to me
so I went and stood by them.
That's the story of how
I befriended the mountains and trees.

I left the mountains behind.
I left the trees behind.
They're where they belong,
and I'm like the wind.
That's the story of how
I said good-bye to the mountains and trees.

## 21. Birds

Regardless of their frailty,
regardless of their splendid feathers,
regardless of the songs they sing,
regardless of the countless poems they've warbled,
regardless even of a pulse
warmed by God's miraculous candlelight....

Regardless of the birds
heavy as a tank
or perfectly monstrous,
indefensibly plain
or damnably ugly...

At the very moment
they unfold their hidden wings
and fly up into the sky,
they become perfect.
The rest is of no consequence.

## 22. A Certain Picture

On a white sketchpad,
see: a yellow birdcage.
The cage door is open
and a long belt of blue sky
sways just beyond.
Inside, with beautiful beaks,
see: two birds.

Perhaps they are going to fly up.
Perhaps they are going to fly up.
Pull on one end of the belt of the bright blue sky;
if it touches the tips of their wings they will fly up.
Will fly up, following the blue of the sky.

Whether they are singing or not
or whispering to each other,
I don't know.
Will they fly or not—
will they stay in their cage?—
I don't know.
A soundless world.
Two birds in a drawing.

Love freely chosen.
Love freely given.
Even should heaven be their birthplace,
and time pass fast as floodwaters,
the two birds inside the cage
are not flying away.
All they do is look at one another.
All they do.

## 23. Toward the West

Everyone:

Whatever it is, who cares?
As a shadow hovers over the ground
and the wind rides the shoulders of that shadow,
so as a black river rises above the wind,
who cares if it's the night?

Who cares if we can't see?
Who cares if the oceans sink farther down
or their waters overflow;
if in the sky above the sky
wild geese fly off honking, *kkei reok, kkei reok,*
or come flying back?
Who cares if we can't see?

Who cares if there's a separation
and sun and moon go their own ways?
If we can never meet?
One thing is certain:
As they sink they fall
together into the west, into the west.

## 24. Sisyphus 1

1

Hi there, Sisyphus.

Though damp be the grass pillow
at the foot of the mountain,
the blue night lays out before you
the ground where you may camp.
Here is that humble place
where you may sleep once the sun goes down,
heavens and earth all in order.

Furious labor
and the pain of repetition:
each wound, each sharp nail punched through logic,
just now is being smoothed over
so that tomorrow, yet again,
a first blood bruise
can arise from skin perfectly new.
Tonight, of course, all should be healed.

Hi Sisyphus.
Stripping off your actionwear
you become but a man with mass
sinking into the loneliness
of his own circumference,
the surrounding silence unending.

## 25. Sisyphus 2

Hi there, Sisyphus.
The rock you feed day after day
with your blood and marrow
senses your touch, like the finest antenna,
in every cell of its body.
Up to this point, it's been alright, but....

If you roll it stealthily from the top of the mountain,
it goes down ahead and waits meekly for you.
Up to this point, that also has been alright, but....

Rock, I am jealous, intensely jealous
of the strength of your beaming confidence
in the inevitability of rescue
and, meantime, the rapture of your waiting.

Most unfair.
In our own, less-than-mythic, world,
once we are separated,
we are forever separated.
Sisyphus, your rock is much too happy.

Even when you two pretend to be apart,
cutting the knot,
that legendary magpie bridge
instantly arcs between you,
a rainbow path,
and I can't stand it.

---

Note: in the classical folk tale "Kyeo-noo Jing-nyeo," the laziness of two lovers led the deities to send them to opposite ends of the Milky Way, the young man on the east condemned endlessly to tend a herd of cows and the young woman on the west condemned endlessly to weave cloth. Finding this punishment too severe, magpies (Korean symbols of good fortune and champions of honest, hardworking folk) took sympathy on the couple. Ever since, on the evening of July 7th of the lunar calendar, all magpies on earth fly up to the Milky Way and form a bridge with their wingtips extending from east to west, so that the two lovers can meet at the middle of the bridge once a year.

## 26. Sisyphus 3

Sisyphus:
For you death is an impossibility,
while we hope to live as long as possible.
In other words, we circle in reverse
the labyrinth of reality and yearning.

However,
through the death that is possible for us,
some have achieved martyrdoms,
some a devotion to pure love.

At an age not far from death,
I realize of a sudden
that even death is a blessing
and dare to worry about you
who can never can die.

Just as one woman did for Jesus,
were I to soak my half-grey hair in perfumed oil
and wash your exhausted body with tears,
perhaps you too could die?

Dear my love Sisyphus,
my heart aches
for one so mighty.

## 27. Sisyphus 4

Even on the first day of snow in the new millennium
he is hiking up the mountain.
A grand seamless quilt of snow
comforts the mountains and fields
and the whole world seems solemn.

Safely reaching the rock,
he starts toward the mountaintop
where no man had set foot since the opening of time,
with only his rock beside him.

On the day
when the karma of his trek was announced,
one of his ribs
was transplanted in the rock
so that, at any movement
the rock comes alive,
reverently lighting his way.
Any time Sisyphus asks,
the rock comes along up the mountain.

The first day it snows in the new millennium
Sisyphus on the mountain
is young and brave, and hardly alone.
Confessing his love, he murmurs,
"My wife, o my wife,"
and brushes away the snow falling on the cold rock.

## 28. Winter River

Winter river frozen over,
its heart long shut
beneath a seamless blanket of ice,
yet there is someone bearing on his shoulders
the burden of a world of frozen snow,
moving his hand over an aching land,
feeling for its pulse.

Who is he, really? Who?
Though his heart be deeply hidden,
it seems like I know he's there.
It seems like I feel
a love so supernally powerful
and caring it never sleeps.
So I surrender myself to him
and desire to serve him all my life
as my elder, that elusive being
whose presence I cannot explain
but in which it seems I believe.

## 29. Pain

They say
that pain fine as the finest gold
can be endured no more than three days.

They say
that during the age of persecution
when Catholics were sentenced to slow death
and hanged by their heels,
in three days
their scalps sweated blood like scarlet dew
and, lapsing into coma,
their pain was vanishingly fine.

Compare to this
a most trifling pain that visited me,
cohabiting for three months.
Having at last discovered
that the seed I had cultivated as religion
was but a shallow imitation,
I gouged it out—
an amateur surgery.
The mysterious sweetness
of the horrifyingly fresh blood
on the tip of the blade
shook me to my bones.

The pain withdrew
to a room known as the subconscious.
When, like a slow IV drip, the bleeding stopped,
many guests visited me at once,
all called "Autumn."
In their company,
after so many stoic years,
my eyes stung
and my tears welled up.

## 30. That Woman

That woman: who envies most the joy
of the grasses and herbs bathing in the sun.

That woman: who knows the midnight wind has come to visit
though the doorknob does not rattle.

That woman: with wings even in her heart
who cannot rest for the flapping
and, though tired, so very tired,
clears the way for old familiars, ancient rivers and mountains,
and sets before them trays of tea.

That woman: who wears out wooden clogs and shoes of straw
walking on through bad weather and good.

That woman: whose finest gifts are pregnancy and parturition.

That woman: who from time to time gives birth
alone in a wide and wild field.

## 31. Flags*

Why are flags so alone?
Towering high,
flapping restlessly
but alone.

Dear friends, you are the flags.
Even when the whole world calls your names
you still head over the steep high peaks of every instant
alone,
spirits of the bird of dawn
soaring into the sky,
shedding fire and dew.

In Seoul, Korea,
halfway between heaven and earth
where the morning opens on the edge of the Eastern sky,
we are a forest of flags
waving with the blood and sweat
of the best of what is human.

Dear friends!
Why are flags solitary and solemn?
Why do we love each other so deeply?

---

*Written for and read aloud at the opening of the Tenth Asian Games in Seoul in 1986.

## 32. Postal Matter

Even to places I cannot go
my book goes with pasted stamps.
On the first page of the book
I write a recipient's name
and for a moment place my cold hands above that name.
I direct my book to arrive and give my warm regards;
to remain quietly at the person's side for a long long time;
and when that recipient is all alone,
to stick evermore faithfully by his side.
Such heartfelt wishes and commands
go along with my book, invisibly, inextricably.

## 33. Solitude

1

Buried, the secret emblem of my joy and sorrow.
Someday, unobserved,
it will sprout

and bloom as a flower of inaudible solitude
to touch, out of the blue,
another's solitude.

2

Like echoes that travel great distances
and return from greater distances—
distances impossibly far—
solitude moves
from one life through the next
and the next,
quietly reincarnate,
taking its place at the head of creation
before all other ranks and offices.

## 34. Pencil Lead

Naked:
I am a naked pencil lead.
But do not try to write with me.
I will snap
and leave you with an empty field of words.

Do not even touch me.
I may poke you.
Standing perilously on end,
I am a blinded thorn.

While I enjoyed days of dreaming
in a robe of juniper,
where did you go?
Where did you go
as my bark-skin flaked away?

Now
the bare touch of a lip is harmful.
Deep black zinc.

I'm a pencil lead.
Even when I snap, it's more than a snap,
it's a spiral of despair,
bit by vanishing bit, *dong-khang, dong-khang*
and I am dumbfounded.

## 35. Concert on the 87th Children's Day, 5 May 2010

Miraculous as a sunrise at sunset:
on Leper Island, Sorokdo,
the London Philharmonia Orchestra, with guest Jo Yong-pil,
gave a concert that unfolded as I read the morning paper.

Beethoven's Symphony No.5 in C minor,
"The Destiny Symphony," was played slowly and ardently,
and so astonishing was the voice of Jo Yong-pil
as he sang "Dear Friend" and "Dream"
backed by a world-renowned orchestra—
so very astonishing—
that the audience of lepers felt excruciating joy.

Confided the Philharmonia's concert master:
"I understand their pain and suffering.
I wanted to convey to them the love of the people of the world
and, if only for a short while,
I wanted to give them the sensation of being on another planet."

Why is this so dizzying?

The world of a sudden swells with a sacred joy so full
that people can go on for days without food or water.

Jo Yong-pil is a star to the lepers of Korea
and Beethoven is unknown,
but no one said a thing.
Rather,
the extraordinary evening came and went,
embraced in its entirety.
Then,
next dawn,
the newspaper came to my doorstep.

---

Note: Jo Yong-pil is the most famous Korean pop singer.

## 36. To My Poem 3

No longer will I
lay you out on my operating table
and cut into you with a scalpel.
My bare hand alone
will catch the pulse of your haggard body.

Nor will I hold to
that silver dagger of virtue
I placed between us
during our time of troubles.
And I will restrain myself
from that cruelty
of rubbing salt into old wounds.

In the expansive forgetfulness of old age,
let us sit side by side
in a dry, congenial wind
and squint toward the faint horizon.

That horizon is now, so to speak,
a friend to be newly recalled,
a teacher for what remains of life.

Dear poem,
in the setting sun
for the first time I feel peaceful.

## 37. Concerning Consolation

I cannot console you.
I cannot punch up the pounding of my heart
to match the desperate spasms of your convulsions.
I cannot, though I pray
as I prepare your food—
        pray from the bottom of my heart—
I cannot put spoon and chopsticks in your hand.

Today, smiling,
I cannot make anyone laugh
nor with some lullaby
lift-lilt anyone
over into dream.

In this world now
consolation's no longer possible.
There must come a carriage
bulging with the seeds of consolation.
Must come a carriage
driven by a fine young coachman.
Must come in droves
*owah owah*
tender-hearted farmers
to do the planting.

If that's not it...
what are we all going to do?

## 38. Train

When the train stopped,
one person stepped out and stood in front of me.

That person
ate a few dishes of my heart
at my dining table
and left again
for his terminal.

After that
sometimes trains stopped in front of me
but no one stepped out.

When time had so passed that a white fog
lay lightly on the brows of my eyes,
I boarded a train
and went to his world,
where he was already waiting
to greet me.

## 39. Someone Who Listens

Your music summons my heart.
For a long time I could endure no more stories
but lately I thirst for the words of others
and have come to attend to your tale.

Our spoken words are clumsy,
our speaking a lonely job.
Indeed, we row for a lifetime,
asea on the nothingness of our words.
Even so, we are creatures who speak,
and should.

Unbundle for me one of the stories
you wish to tell.
Plant the seeds of trees and flowers in my soil.
I assure you of a good pruning
and careful trimming in the times ahead.

Today
as one who sits before you, listening,
I feel sweet.

## 40. South Gate (Sungnye)

*Are you just passing through? Are you doing alright?*
So warmly does Sungnye see us off,
looking after each of us until we're faint specks down the road. . . .
Ahhh, how gracious is Sungnye,
great king of farewells,
eldest brother of the palace gates,
ranking elder of National Treasures—
and how bitterly painful our love:
suddenly (I can't believe it)
Sungnye's six-hundred-year-old body went up in flames,
and though that typhoon of fire might be honored as immolation,
its sacred skeleton was rescued,
the spirit of history racing full-steam toward the arson
faster than any punishment from heaven.
Weeping,
flakes of our skin falling like ash,
we wrap Sungnye's bones in sheet upon sanctified sheet
of rice paper.

Dear immortal Sungnye,
you of the limitless heart
and miraculous powers of resurrection,
you scrape away fire-scar and brush off the ashes.

May you become a gate of cures and blessings,
healing wounds and heartache across the world.

May you live as long as God,
with a beginning and no end.

---

Note: Sungnye, the ancient name for South Gate, at the center of Seoul, is the Number 1 Korean National Treasure.

## 41. The Twentieth Century

I loved the Twentieth Century.

I met my life as my betrothed
and through my life-studies
(fated to begin most miserably
on fields of war and death)
I was awakened to pure and passionate yearning
and the nobility of life.

I loved the Twentieth Century.
I loved its shuddering, suffering, and trembling hope.
I loved the sublime loneliness of my contemporaries,
those talented people, distant as stars
and quite as beautiful,
with their superabundant civilizations
and deeply thoughtful intellectual traditions.
I felt greatly honored
to be graced by their light.

I loved the Twentieth Century.
I loved its aesthetics of heart-numbing contrition,
its shame and the ache of its wounds
and ah, its floods of bitter grief:
"Yes, I did wrong, I did wrong."

I ever so much loved the Twentieth Century
whose lessons and blood, now transfused
into a new millennium, reverberate
through the deepest of nerves.

## 42. Sunset

Praying, the setting sun
leaves its throne.
This is the sun's inner flash,
the burning fragrance of its flame
and its shimmering,
an ocean of fire, of heartfelt repentance.
Souls
thrown fearlessly into that flame
are forged
like a crimson bar of metal.

The sunset follows in behind,
holding open an unimpeachable book
whose letters only the new-tempered can read.

## 43. To Myself

1

If you want to go, let's go.
Stepping across a thousand knifeblades,
let's go up to the summit covered perpetually with snow.
There, you and I,
let's fight to the death.

More to the point
than just risking our lives,
let's do battle
for the truth of love—
or what amounts to the soul.
Could we truly love, if not desperately?
Could we truly live, if not so desperately?

If you want to go, let's go.
Even in the mid-day sun,
clouded with the dense smoke of gunpowder:
let's get on with it.

2

Your right is forfeit,
like a student in an examination room
who may not resubmit an answer sheet.
You used up your one chance
and got your grade:
you could not make one man happy,
and this applies correspondingly
to the rest.

From now on,
you and remorse must share a cell
and serve out the time
to which you sentenced yourself.
To be precise:
in this world you never have a second chance
to hold out your hand.

## 44. Sleep

He sleeps so deeply
that today as well he does not wake.

The stone walls of the house of sleep are so solid
that I may call it a solemn palace,
and after closing a pair of gates
I may call myself a faithful gatekeeper.

O dear eyelid of soundest sleep:
Peace is endless,
and the Elder in charge of the universe
clothes him with the divine blessing of sleep,
such that his sleep becomes deeper and deeper,
no need for lullaby.

His sleep is heavy,
the peace of his sleep
like a wide ocean.

I salute the divine blessing of sleep.
Until the time comes that I too fall asleep,
I who worship sleep
keep its vigil.

## 45. Desert

1
Never have I met
such a serious man.

Since Genesis,
this one mulishly stubborn bachelor
has lived alone, like God,
a-tremble with enormous vitality
and honing a knifeblade, *seureuk, seureuk*,
in the sands of desert winds.

2
Just now
for the first time in this world
I am received by perfect silence.

Just now
before the transcendent and eternal
I am received by the oldest brother of the finest bloodline.

Just now
waiting on the guillotine and the fragrance of the dew
I am received by martyr upon martyr.

## 46. Desert 9

Vastness, trembling with fear.
From ancient times to the present,
the territory of the unattached,
of those without partners, god-sends;
this desert.

Were these, bodies or souls of the unattached,
slipped in between heaven and earth like thin sheets of paper
they would shudder, *peollung, peollung,* empty and lonely.
"Everyone is alone"
would echo loudly across the high plains, *oorung, oorung.*
Each one someone else's painful fragment or remnant:
a fatedness dark to us
who cannot put our fingers on
the whole of a life.

I'm afraid of the desert.
I'm truly afraid
of the absoluteness of outright arrogance and cruelty.
But, O desert!
Under your sky
those without god-sends are absolutely your children.

## 47. To Winter Again

Are all of these
shining letters
your book,
Winter?

Common sense says
that people who sleep underground
may go easily without bread,
while people who walk the surface
must clear their hearts
by cleaning away their words.

Cry it does
but the winter river makes no sounds;
its tears flow beneath crystal
and the winds
stumble across sharp ice.

Should cold things long
to embrace each other,
Mother Earth enfolds them all,
compassionate.

Should the sun set,
a person who sleeps underground
may go on easily without a lamp
and a person who walks the surface
beneath the stars has light aplenty.
I awaken to find that he and I
are together under the same blanket
in the wide expanse of time and space.

Are these painfully bright
beaming letters
all in your book,
Winter?

## 48. Pocket Diary of Grief

1.
I know the mind that departs for distant seas.
I know the mind that arrives alone at a village
        deep in a mountain valley.
I know also the mind that returns along a distant remembered road
to hear news of the people of the world.

2.
Hey man, you there, ringing the bell,
crying and pummeling.
In order to sound the bells clearly
throughout the nine heavens,
how many tens of thousands of times
must people wail
and the bells shout out?

3.
I am going upstairs.
When I go up endlessly and reach the top
I find darkness: clouds.
I am going downstairs.
When I go down endlessly and reach the bottom
I find clouds: darkness.
At this I realize
that stairtop and stairbottom are the same.

4.
Illness came to me as if a guest.
It entered and sat by my head, saying,
"It's been a long time."
It opens an enormous book and shows me
written characters,
witness to what's going on in the world.
I gaze at them and recall the chill
like sipping ice water.
My tears fall strangely sweet.

5.
As one knows the real meaning of a meal
only when starving,
only one who has suffered a loss knows
the significance of loss.
The extract of hardship is sweetness.

Oh, dear separation!
Let all remaining truths
sink into the depths of the ocean.

6.
Prayer is the devotion
of people speaking truth to heaven.
Today our truth is darkness,
so we are devoting the darkness to you.
Grace is what is given
to people from heaven;
if that surplus of things in heaven
is today's darkness, please,
may you pour more darkness down upon us.

7.
She who has been shocked,
whose body is so electric
she cannot bear the touch of wind or air. . . .
arms, shuddering arms, arms
approaching from winter fields
and waves of arms, *wa wa,*
from the empty air,
coming to grasp her.

8.
I will lose him.
No one can change this sequence.
All other things remain as they were, fixtures
in my life, except for this inevitable fact,
which came to me as a flying mane of wind.
Look, up there!
Just before my eyes.
Now,
the sky is falling. Falling.

9.

For tossing my prayer into the mud
I forgive You.
In turn I am grateful for all You have forgiven me.
Today, however, I am most profusely sorry, God.
I shall forgive You.

O, You who can never be in error must be in error,
and I a rebel against the regime.

Heaven being closed,
it's no use to pray from the bottom of my heart and soul.
Anyhow, at times like this, weeping is pointless.

10.

From the indeterminateness of ancient times
I kept walking
and today, at last, arrived here,
where there's nowhere left to go,
and nothing more can happen: the last land,
that is, pure longing.

## 49. Learning Something New

I guess I could learn the magic.
An ancient white kerosene lamp
hangs among cobwebs.
*Seol seol:* stirring boiling water black as ink
in a fairytale cauldron large as a bathtub,
grandmother witch thinks something's missing
and adds more strange herbs
while drawing up two lists
she keeps close to her bosom,
those she will punish
and those she must help,
reciting spell after spell
in syllables wetter than the sound of rain.

I guess I could learn the magic
and become a fervent disciple of grandmother witch,
who does many wonderful things
and stirs handfuls of beneficent herbs
into the black ink of the cauldron,
drawing me into her grand arcana.

In my youth,
after seeing a circus girl riding a horse,
the entire world seemed to glow as if at sunset,
and now, in these lonely times,
I would like to feel again that envy and excitement.

I guess I could learn the magic.

## 50. The News

So long as I was alive
I would have forgiven you
anything at all, a thousand times over,
had you remained alive.

You did nothing wrong
but the very thing
I begged you not to do:
bull's-eye!
an arrow straight to the heart of the taboo, *peong!*

. . . Devastating news.

## 51. To Despair

Dear despair, let's travel together.
Vowing to honor the directive to despair all the way to the end
and not to separate even after we've reached the end,
let the two of us go along with quiet affection.

When we tire of traveling by foot,
let's go piggyback, each riding the other in turn.
At night, ever unable to fall asleep
because our eyes burn like fireballs,
let's pretend at least to sing
lullabies to one another.

As time passes, despair too grows into adulthood,
and once adult, ages until finally it dies.
So be it: there's no option, I guess,
but to take up the unfinished work
and, reaching maturity,
despair ever more zealously
as I grow slowly older and die.

## 52. Sedan

A small house,
its strong roof warding off rain and wind,
its walls on all sides glass.
Before me a painted scroll
unfolds without wrinkles;
street lamps in straight lines shine
like gold buttons.
For a while now, here
in the middle of this vast city
where the fog is thick with melancholy and loneliness,
you and I have shared this house.
Inside, I link arms with melancholy,
the melancholy of the crestfallen.
One day, I may want to write
a letter to this address.

## 53. To Sorrow

Is silence locked in?

Shut the door, pull the red cloth over:
within the casket, unfamiliar silence.

I offer as a cradle
this strange time, night without day,
and this strange place,
seams of darkness overlapping.
Rock it slowly, gently, *neuriit, neuriit.*
and, please, make no noise.

Instead, give birth
to a child whose jade-white skin
is so warm it makes one weep
the jewel-tear of *sarira.*
Why not? Let me be witness to that birth.

My dear blind sorrow!

---

Note:
*sarira:* a small crystal sometimes bound in with the ashes of a Buddhist monk and regarded as a sacred relic.

## 54. Ascension

"I will show you
a woman who dies for love."
On the t.v. screen
a despondent woman dies, instantly.

On its own, a single bullet exploded,
breaking free from its shell.
That woman won the dare
I had abjured
and sued the coward within me,
sentencing without trial, putting to death.

Then
at her command
came a passing shower the color of fresh peaches
and she ascended in a golden light.

## 55. Still Life

The boat in the picture
floats on a painted wave.
A boat so dazzlingly white
that the indigo light rising from the depths
of the boundless expanse of painted water
cannot turn its reflection blue.

Behind the glass wall
of the frame, a figure
does not age with the passing of time.

Earlier, silver push pins
had stilled the beating of his heart
and with a heart so deeply asleep,
ah, the silence is overwhelming.

Boat and figure
command this corner of the house
where one woman, a far-traveler
all her long life, passes by
streaming with the ichor of pain.

## 56. The Letter

I've never known anyone I could love more than you.
No one has so kept me to the path of righteousness.
I weep each time I think these thoughts.

No one has ever led me to be so honest.
You are the clearest of mirrors, reflecting what lies within me.
If I could make my way through your depths,
I would find myself, eyes tearful,
at my own beginning.

I write to you every day.
The moment I compose a single phrase,
you are already here, reading the words.
This letter, therefore,
need never be mailed.

## 57. True Love

Mrs. Pearl Buck, the American writer,
had an only daughter who was simple,
an imbecile, a sister of Nature,
like wind or wave.

When the daughter was about forty,
she often listened to music
at her sanitarium on the beach.
She nodded occasionally to classical music
but shook her head fretfully
at the sound of jazz.

Mrs. Pearl Buck, in her saddest of books,
The Child Who Never Grew,
marveled at her daughter,
whom she described as follows:
"She has an extraordinary integrity of character....
She is a child of great purity."

That must be true love,
its sadness deep enough to unhinge the earth
yet beyond one hears the song of a mother's love,
*O merciful beauty,*
*O merciful beauty,*
*Dear merciful beauty*
a song that plays on and on.

## 58. A Certain Boy

Like a delivery of fresh flowers
a boy came to my ward.
I told him, "I feel just now like I'm in prison."
He said, "Wherever I am
is a wasteland and desert."
Surprised, I answered,
"You should be more of an optimist."
He said, "That's worse than pessimism,
since profligate, moronic, and wearying."

Child,
have you already looked down
from the brink of thousand-foot cliffs?
Have you ever surrendered—
blue with anger, fear, and grief,
the nerves of your body gone numb—
raising both hands into the air?

Worse,
how does someone
who has mined your heart
take on wings, leave your body,
and fly away?

. . . O child.

## 59. Children

I call them “children,” all
the still-snarled threads
of old entanglements,
foreordained but unresolved:
Children who hurt themselves,
children with lots to talk about,
wordless children,
children who fail to grow up
or who age too quickly.
Wherever their lives verge on the tragic,
it’s my fault I gave them flesh and bone.
A mom’s fault.

My children.
My children.
Yet again: my children.

## 60. Food Chain

Out in the ocean hundred of meters deep,
pods of killer whales hunt for food at high speed,
fierce predators tackling even other whales.
Like soldiers in a chow line,
each takes just one bite
before yielding to the next.

They say that the bodies of these orca
average four meters long, their lifespan sixty years.
Their favorite prey are baby seals
just weaned from their mothers' breasts.
Orca swallow them in a single gulp
then violently spout water.
As if slashed by a swift knife,
the silence of the ocean is unseamed.

In a flash,
as I was watching the t.v. program,
my skin began to crawl.

I thought about God, who created every living thing
and released us all from our captivity
to bear the round burden of eating
and being eaten.

## 61. Toying with Self-Reproach

I reproach myself;
the truth is that I am tired.
I reproach myself;
my skin bloats with laziness, indolence.
I reproach myself—
a really sweet way of killing time.

I reproach myself.
Tepidity is what this is, a way of diffusing the tension,
of despairing as only one can
who has zero-personality.

I reproach myself.
My habit of self-reproach
subserves a master calendar
of exacting dates of reproach.
My days and nights are occupied
with this, my toying with self-reproach,
since I don't have many years left for toying.
Ergo and therefore, I am very busy
furiously reproaching myself.

## 62. Vista

Spirit of midsummer
that had flopped down
    all sweaty
now rises and lopes off.
The trees remain, as always.

At hazy sunset
    birds returning to their nests
        wing across the sky
and the wind sounds just within the outer gate
        *swah swah swah.*
In that moment the trees
wash and rinse their hair
and bow together toward Vespers.

When music is playing for the Mass
and the Lord's Prayer is being chanted
and sheets of darkness rise one over the other
across far reaches of sky,
our hearts hold each other
brighter than candles.

Dewdrops falling through the night
wash our heartskin clean.

As day breaks, it dawns on me: autumn is upon us.

## 63. In Honor of Peace

Walk in peace.
Walk in peace.

Listening to Fauré's *Requiem*
I shed a tear even in sunlight.

The winter sun
ushers all of her children
onto a field of ice.

O, compassionate Mother!

Walk in peace.
Walk plentifully in peace.

The coldness of the living
is warmed at the fire
of a requiem mass.

Let me make this clear:
Those who are alive,
those who have passed on,
and those who are yet to be
all are sisters in the Spirit.

Walk in peace

## 64. My Words

My words unfortunately are not dangerous.
None today was shocked by them
nor suffered great pain.

My words ask me,
at sixty and more,
to wait, sealed in time,
until each grape becomes wine.

If a person cannot expess everything,
(so my words tell me)
silence suffices,
and words themselves may bow
under the lightest of winds,
which is most fortunate.

## 65. Rain

Tonight, my kinder years
have been falling away
as the rain streams down in buckets.

Rain sinks rivulet by rivulet to the bottom of Time.
Stirring the current,
I undo and rewrite
its characters.

I had wanted to commit one endearing sin,
planning to share with only one person
that karma which will not be worked off
in this world or the Other,
or through eons of afterworlds....

Alas.
Even such a sin is out of reach when fate does not conspire with you.
I wash my hands in the rain.

Should I raise my voice in praise?
Should I raise my voice in praise?
Today, should I praise the rain
soaking so deeply into the marrow of my bones?
I should.
A hot-blooded woman should
at the very least
do us all the courtesy of dying young.

## 66. Sky

Those who feel sad are in luck:
each day that they sorrow
their stomachs fill with sadness
and they forget all other hungers.

Those who love are in luck:
they know the end.
At the end
one person leaves
ahead of the other.

On that day the remnant look up.
No more rhetorical flourishes.
Just call it "sky."

## 67. Port

Months gone and long adrift
in my single willow leaf of a boat,
the bow brushes past the shore
and again I am away.

If I'd met up here with someone in need of solace
or someone warmhearted, with sad eyes,
I'd have disembarked,
abandoning my boat
at water's edge,
letting it float off
across the boundless expanse

## 68. On the Unavailing

I am giving you a handful of keys
with which you can open my heart and mind.
You may also, if you wish, open
any locked room, drawer, or vault.

You can have anything
then.
After you have what you want,
if you would like to fill an empty bowl
with the crumbs of an empty sky,
you can do so.

Among us,
some give,
some receive.
Spurning what you are given,
or letting it go to seed,
call this, when given, unavailing;
when received, indifference.
The unavailing happens every day.
We are, so to speak, sustained by futility.

I have chosen you
as partner in my futility.
I love you.

## 69. Songs of Solomon 4

Loneliness
from the deepest roots
to the crown of the head.
O, I must share only with thee
that from its origins in the east to its vanishing
beyond the rim of the west,
the seam that runs endlessly
along the heavens
as they revolve and revolve
returns ever to this heart.

## 70. Earth

I wish to be like Mother Earth.

Should you come back and sow
after years away, even then
Mother Earth will offer up her fruits
with all their flavors and nutrients.
Should you dig a well, water will come.
And should you die, you will sleep deeply,
so deeply, embraced
with caresses and quiet lullabies.
Such an amazing motherhood.

People:
Would we were all like that.

## 71. White Angel

Said to be a mystery all its own: the white angel.
In that fleeting moment when
you make out its entire body, white as snow,
you wonder: mirage or dream?
At the best of times
in this world of ours it may be
the very glory of the eyes.
That vision, however, should be kept a secret
as absolute as the hidden plans of Providence.
Heaven otherwise would be unhinged.

I hope with all my heart to see the white angel at least once.
And to see the man who was transformed by the white angel.
In this world where so much is surprising
that no one is easily surprised,
I would burst in upon everyone,
set them aflame with the joy
of my shouting:
"I have seen the white angel,
I have seen the white angel!"

I want wildly to wave the firebrand of astonishment.
I want to strike all of the sleeping bells across the planet
so that I can fill the world with their ringing.

I who at sixty
am starved for something new
would welcome, oh yes welcome, the outrage
that would come of such a sacrilege
as laying bare the secret of the heavens.

## 72. The Dining Table of the New Millennium

In the New Millennium
the prayer is the same as before.
Grace the bread of our table,
leavened with love
and toasted in a holy flame
so that our hearts become as delicious bread
to share with each other.
Grace the cup of our table
with a layer of dew
from the spring that gushes at dawn
and let us toast each other
so that our hearts are as pure water.

There are, within Creation,
things visible, the flux of time, and
things that are invisible,
blood circulating, pulses beating.
Grace us with the vision to see,
veiled as if in dreams,
the master of bread and wine,
esteemed father of the Universe
sitting always at the head of the table.

## 73. The Present Situation

Music sprawls
alone in a back room of my house.
That music, having matured,
will be peaceful only in His presence.

Yet the Peace is incomplete.
What else is left to me
but one painfully cold heart
rattling in the throws of an icy die
with at most a clumsy gift of gab
and whatever penalty that incurs.

Today too I exchanged one golden day
for a handful of sand,
and now at sunset
I feel those strange single sheets of cellophane
clinging transparent to my skin.

My sin
is wishing to speak grandly
about will o' the wisps that appear and disappear
in the hidden leaves of books:
the other selves of my spirit
returning from their excursions.

A solemn thought now occurs to me:
at this age I should become a pupil
of perfected stillness and fallow calm.

## 74. A Guest from Afar

A guest is coming from afar.
I don't know where he came from
or when he started out,
but he's headed steadily toward my door.
I suppose he'll be neither cold like winter
nor wild like storm.
I suppose he'll hold my hand
with as much grace and affection as estimable age,
saying in a comforting tone, "I'm here.
I trust I arrived at a good time."

This notable guest,
the one I can't see,
is headed steadily this way,
gently erasing the landscape as he passes,
like fog or hazy moonlight.

Oh, I so wish
that he and I come to understand
each other in our deepest parts
when we do (and we *do*) meet. . . .

## 75. Confession

1
I broke the silence.
I had lived bent over
under a sin sweet and wide as heaven.
A lone man
gone to embrace the sinking sun,
escorted by a lone shadow
and a single gust of wind—
never seen again.

2
Her love,
he forgave;
his not loving,
she forgave as well—
if vice-versa,
still they would have forgiven each other.
For as long as we live,
ah, let us be lonely in just that way.

## 76. Confession 2

Finally: done.
My confession of love
became buckshot and scattered
as if a flower had bloomed and withered:
so natural, and such a relief—
my last unrequited love
to be set down
on life's résumé
is hereby complete.

## 77. Chair

As each of us,
among the billions of this world,
has a distinct destiny,
so also the fate of each of the many winds
among updrafts and downdrafts
has its own affidavit.

Consider
a wind that has blown in from the beginning of the world,
and this very day
might fold its wings right in front of me,
right in front of me.
I want to befriend that wind in particular.
I mean no longer to go forward on the path of life.

Life is walking one's road, isn't it?
Everyday I have walked my road
and I have come to this point, here.
So now I want to know I have arrived
and be seated in a chair.

I who have walked for sixty years,
would like to take a seat for the next sixty
with my spiritual guide beside me,
a wind scarcely finished with its work.
I would sit and meditate,
waiting for my secret orders.

## 78. High Plains

Today is almost gone
and I'm utterly ashamed of my life.
I'd planned to arrive at a poem
but my words and their meanings lie in tatters.
And just now it occurs to me it has been too long
since I visited the high plains.

That place where the tall winds wait,
passing the time back and forth,
and attend upon the horizon, speechless
for as long as it takes...
that place to which, one way or another,
I return as something of an adult.

The half of my face turned
toward life
burns with its heat.

In this era,
north south east or west,
which master now admonishes us
not to surrender our souls,
and instructs us in the strictest of precepts—
not to throw away our lives, not to yield;
to resist even unto death?

So I,
who could not speak of love
apart from the migraine of anguish,
passed easy lazy days dozing off,
mired in the quicksand of the half-asleep
and in mortal danger, held in the grip
of a monologue as deep as it was dark.

I really must go to the high plains
to hold still among the hulking winds
and look across in long silences
to the wide horizon.

Every last part of me should go—
eyes, head, heart,
and spirit too,
exhausted, prostrate—
myself entire.
There.

## 79. Speaking to the Wind

Who says that wind is invisible?

The murmuring of leaves
is the silhouette of the wind.

Undulations at river's edge
are figures of the wind.

All directions, front, back, left, right, are its guests,
living together with the wind.

I say to the wind:
*I have already lived well for a long time,*
*and today my eyes are still bright, my ears still keen.*
*I am humbled and overwhelmed with gratitude.*

I say to the wind:
*In the coming days, I shall leave behind debts of kindness.*
*Accept in advance my apologies for favors I cannot repay.*

Having lived only with the wind,
there can be no other heir.

## 80. Warm Music

I shall go to his house,
across oceans and farther yet,
where the powder of time has fallen
so long it has become a deep lucent snow.
He shall sit in a chair
and, as a child does,
I shall sit on his lap.
Setting the weight of one's life on the altar
each anniversary of passing,
the whole world shall be still.
Amid flowing tears
I shall come to the end of tears.

Finally I shall bid farewell,
and accompanied by the warmest music
return to my reserved seat.
Hereafter
the music shall always, always be playing.

## 81. On the Shore of the Han in Winter

O, winter river,
the notes of your music are endless.
Today a dark blue skein of thread
lies on the bed beneath the icy river,
alarming and beautiful.
Were someone possessed
and swept away beneath the freezing water,
what could I do?

Perhaps a passing boat
sent splinters of ice down the river;
an old bleached-out ferry?
Perhaps there was a man on the ferry
whose long coat flapped in the driving winds, *soguk-soguk*.
Ice floes crunched alongside the boat.
"Halloo! Halloo!"
Somebody may have been chasing after him.

I recall a Japanese movie I saw when I was young:
a grey-haired father took on his back
a bleeding daughter
who had put a dagger in her heart.
"Halloo! Halloo!
Stop! Stop, I beg of you!"
The father kept on running as he called out to her young man
who had set off in a boat.
I'm sure everyone has known such a boat
pushing off in grief.
Indeed, everyone has cried out after such a boat,
"Hold on! Hold on!"

O, winter river,
I wish that all of my farewells might gather in reunion.
I wish for a dancefloor on which to dance the circle dance
*gang-gang-su-weollae gang-gang-su-weollae.*
Better still were a full moon to rise into the night.

## 82. Silence

Now I would like to put away words.
Tell all the words and tears
grown old after several hundreds of years,
tell them: go and rest; yes, go and rest.
On this day of heavy spring rain
from a watering can as vast as the heavens,
I would like to say good-bye.

I would like to wave off
that bird that sang throughout the winter
and sang also at the grave.
That bird and its song could go on,
it seems, for hundreds of years,
its throat wide and open,
but I would say: dear bird, dear song,
fly, yes, fly away.

I would like everything that sounds
in my sky
to drift down with the sunset
and a single undefiled silence
be the sturdy dolmen, the stone marker
of the rest of my life.

## 83. To Hope

Do as you wish.
I didn't even notice your coming
and already you want to leave.
Do as you wish.
Take care on your way out.

In the wide wind-tossed world,
while you turn and spin
like a whirligig,
I would be ever so grateful
for the scrap of a letter.

If, oh my god,
you appeared someday like a ghost
whom time and tide have endlessly filled and emptied,
after no farewell and not a single letter,
yes, yes, I would still be glad, so very glad.

Glad even should nothing of the sort happen
but on the last day of my life
you were finally to come to me,
when I'd tell you that an ardent farewell
at the close of my life
is not too late;
is early.